Family Online Research

"How to Spend Little or No Money and Find your Ancestors"

By Sam Maner
2018

Table of Continence

How to Find What You Are Looking For
And
Not Waste Your Money

Sam Maner
Email: sr1776@yahoo.com
Phone 865-386-7272

http://tnresearcher1779.wix.com/tennesseeresearcher

Password for Heritage Quest 1003_ _ _ _ _   Numbers
Password for Fold 3   User Name tnresearcher1779@gmail.com
Password   history101

Research Places to Check First

familysearch.org Search and Wiki

Heritage Quest (Open from my site in new page)

Ancestry
(Free Records)
Social Security, 1940 Census, 1880 Census

Find a Grave

genealogytrails.com

legacy family tree

Archives.org

Google Books

Google Search

Genealogy.com (Don't Pay for the site)

The Library has access to Ancestry.com for 5.00 fee

Pay Sites that are worth the money

WARNING USE A PRE PAID CARD

Ancestry
Fold3
Newspaers.com

Sites not to trust and not worth the money

GenealogyBank.com

My Heritage

DO NOT PUT YOUR GENEALOGY ON ANCESTRY

Here's why
http://familyhistorydaily.com/genealogy-help-and-how-to/the-huge-genealogy-mistake-we-all-need-to-stop-now/

Basic Research Information (Brief)

How do I begin?
• Start with what you know which means starting with yourself and work backwards.
• Find as much information as you can about your parents, grandparents, and more distant ancestors. Write the information down.
• Always include maiden names for females, if known. Females will be listed under that name until they were married.
• Include dates and places of births, marriages, and deaths and include the places your ancestors lived between their birth and death, if known. You should always use continental dating (DD MMM YYYY where DD is the day of the month,
MMM is the 3 letter abbreviation of the month, and YYYY is the year. For example, 03 Mar 1897 would be March 3,1897.). Place names should be written in the following format: City or Town, County, State, such as Durant, Bryan County, Oklahoma.
• Talk to or write other family members. They often have information or documentation you need. Another family member may also be working on your family tree.
• Record your information on forms referred to as family group sheets and pedigree charts. Indicate a source for each fact. Organize your information so that you can locate an individual in your growing collection of information.

Where do I find the information I need?
• At home: Sources of information include birth certificates, marriage licenses, death certificates, divorce decrees, newspaper clippings, family bibles, diaries, and letters.
• Local and state government offices: A state's Bureau of Vital Statistics can be contacted for copies of birth and death certificates. Records that can be found at a county courthouse include marriage, divorce, land, deeds, and wills (probate). Cemetery records are also sometimes useful.
• Most libraries have books on how to do genealogical research. They also will have books on the history of the area.
Most large city libraries have an area dedicated to genealogy. Many university libraries also have genealogical and historical collections available to researchers.
• Genealogical and historical societies, both local and state, are good sources for information. Many have copies of county school records, family histories, censuses, old newspapers, cemetery records, and funeral home records, etc.
• The Church of Jesus Christ of Latter Day Saints (Mormon) Family History Library has "branch" locations called Family History Centers at many of their local facilities. The Family History Library contains a large collection of genealogical documents that may be useful in research. Their Family search website has many documents online (www.familysearch.org).
• Records available through the National Archives in Washington, D.C. and the National Archives' regional branches include federal census records from 1790 – 1930, special censuses of various Indian tribes, military and service related records, and passenger arrival records. National Archives website is www.archives.gov.
• The Internet: Several websites, such as Rootsweb (www.rootsweb.com) and Family Search have online guides that give helpful information about how and where to search. Rootsweb and Ancestry.com (www.ancestry.com) also allow people to post their family trees. You may find some of your ancestors included in someone else's tree. Also posting information from your own family tree may provide a link for others that are researching another branch of the same family.

Understanding How to Search
For Names
Last Name Spellings

- Smith, Smyth, Smif
- Germans Changing Names **(ex. Zimmerman = Carpenter)**
- French Name Changes
- Census Takers Spellings
- Missed First name error
- Ancestry Errors

Name Searching Census

- Use of first 3 letters and *
- Or * and last 3 letters
- First Name Search
- Location Search
- Other Sources
  - Tax Records
  - City Directories

Marriage Records

- The dreaded initials
- Finding maiden names and going back
- Marriage records with birth info !!
- Finding if the marriage is online
  - Not all records are online
  - Some are different places

Death Certificate

- Finding if they are online
  - http://www.deathindexes.com/
- Most States start full time 1914-present
- How to understand what you have.

Land Records and Court Cases
Church Records
Other Crazy places to look

- Other Counties close by
- County Histories
- State Court Cases
- Federal Court Cases

PEDIGREE CHART

CHART NO.

NO. 1 ON THIS CHART

IS THE SAME AS NO. ______

ON CHART NO. ______

8 GREAT- GRANDFATHER
CONTINUED ON CHART ______
BORN
WHERE
MARRIED
WHERE
DIED
WHERE

9 GREAT- GRANDMOTHER
CONTINUED ON CHART ______
BORN
WHERE
DIED
WHERE

4 GRANDFATHER
BORN
WHERE
MARRIED
WHERE
DIED
WHERE

10 GREAT- GRANDFATHER
CONTINUED ON CHART ______
BORN
WHERE
MARRIED
WHERE
DIED
WHERE

11 GREAT- GRANDMOTHER
CONTINUED ON CHART ______
BORN
WHERE
DIED
WHERE

5 GRANDMOTHER
BORN
WHERE
DIED
WHERE

2 YOUR FATHER
BORN
WHERE
MARRIED
WHERE
DIED
WHERE

12 GREAT- GRANDFATHER
CONTINUED ON CHART ______
BORN
WHERE
MARRIED
WHERE
DIED
WHERE

13 GREAT- GRANDMOTHER
CONTINUED ON CHART ______
BORN
WHERE
DIED
WHERE

6 GRANDFATHER
BORN
WHERE
MARRIED
WHERE
DIED
WHERE

1 YOU
BORN
WHERE
MARRIED
WHERE
DIED
WHERE

YOUR SPOUSE
NAME OF SPOUSE

14 GREAT- GRANDFATHER
CONTINUED ON CHART ______
BORN
WHERE
MARRIED
WHERE
DIED
WHERE

15 GREAT- GRANDMOTHER
CONTINUED ON CHART ______
BORN
WHERE
DIED
WHERE

7 GRANDMOTHER
BORN
WHERE
DIED
WHERE

3 YOUR MOTHER
BORN
WHERE
DIED
WHERE

PREPARED BY:

DATE:

OK
I've Reached 1850
Now What

What the Census marks mean for 1820-1840

- First Bold Section (MALES) Under 5/ 5-10/10-15/15-20/20-30/30-40/50-60/60 70/70-80/80-90/100-plus
- Second Bold Section (Females) Same Age breakdown.
- Third Bold Section (Free Males of Color)
- Fourth Bold Section (Females of Color)
- Written in at the End (Pensioner)
  - Page 2 Slaves Agriculture

Other Places to Look

- Wills & Probates and Dispersion's of Estates
  - Land Records
  - Bible Records
  - Military Records
- Death Certificates of other Children (See familysearch.org)
  - Tax Records
  - City Directories
  - Newspapers
- Secondary Sources
- Preponderance of Evidence

Wills, Probates Dispersion's of Estates

- Sometimes not all children are listed in the will.
  - Reasons for not being in the will
    - Deceased Child (May list Widow or Widower of)
    - Moved to another state
    - Already given land
    - If there were older children and a second marriage by the deceased
    some times they would list them and give them a dollar to avoid
    contest.
  - Probate is proof of death if you do not have death date they
  will give you a date (Between) Writing o the Will and Probate
  or reporting to the court.

Land Record

- Deeds (Proof of Child or Spouse)
  - With Love and affection I give
  - If there is no charge for the land
    - Survey
  - Land belonging to his decd. Father or Mother or Grandparents.
- Land Grants: Most States have complete applications for

land Oregon required an application to travel there you had

to provide marriage records and locations as well as birth

records. Be sure and check each State.

Bible Records

- **Places to Look**
  - DAR Library (dar.org)GRS
  - National Archives
  - State Archive
  - Local Libraries and Historical Libraries and Museums
- Verify Birth and Deaths

Military Records

- **Wars (If your ancestor is alive during these times)**
  - *French and Indian Wars Dunsmores War 1698-1775*
    - UnPesioned But King Land Grants
  - *Revolutionary War* 1775-1783 Pensioned
- **Indian Wars may also be listed as Old Wars**
  - *Chickamagua Wars 1776-1795*
  - *Northwest Indian Wars 1785-1793*
  - *Whiskey Rebellion 1791-1794*
  - *Quasi War 1798-1800*
  - *First Barbary War 1801-1805*
  - *Tecumseh's War 1811*

— —

War of 1812 (1812-1815
- **Old Wars**
  - *Creek War 1813-1814*
  - *Second Barbary War 1815*
  - *First Seminole War 1817-1818*
  - *Texas Indian Wars 1820-1875*
  - *Arikara War 1823*
  - *Winnebago Wars 1827*
  - *Black Hawk Wars 1832*
  - *Second Seminole War 1835-1842*

— —

Mexican American War 1846-1848

—

- **Pensions**
  - [Non Pay] Heritage Quest (Keep in mind theirs are condensed)
  - [Paid] Fold 3 Full Files

Death Certificates

- Check other children in the family even if your ancestor died before the death certificates some of their brothers and sisters may have lived and give mothers maiden name.
- Check the Cemeteries they are buried in on findagrave.com

Tax Records

- If there is not a Will or Probate find the last time
they are listed in the Tax records. Then use that
as a death date because they either dead or
moved. Always put c.1800 or Abt. 1880 if you
do not know the death date.
- Be sure and look at Pole. If the members of the
household; males are over 18; each one over
18 pay pole.

City Directories

- Most larger towns have directories
  - http://www.uscitydirectories.com
  - All working family members are listed in the
    directory by address
  - Directories give location of where they are working
    and then check the directory for the company they
    may have a add.

Newspapers

- Obituaries Be sure and look several months past the death if they were not close to town it may take as much as 3 months to get in the paper.
- If they were traveling or had visitors they may mention brothers or sisters coming for a visit.
- Check larger towns close to where they were living sometimes they will be listed. Obits or Marriages.

Secondary Sources

- Church Records
- Store books (Accounts) State or County
  Archives
- Court Cases (Check neighbors)
- County Histories
- Preponderance of Evidence

OK
I've Found My Immigrant
NOW WHAT!

England

- National Archive at Kew Gardens

nationalarchives.gov.uk

- Books and Records
- Census
- Freebmd.org.uk
- Death & Birth Records
- Findagrave.com

Ireland-Scotland

- Scotland

Scottishpeople.gov.uk
Scottish Genealogical Society
rsgs.org

- Ireland

Emeraldancestors.com

- Irishgenealogy.ie
https://registers.nli.ie/

Germany-France

- Germany
  - www.jewishgen.org/
  - www.germangenealogygroup.com/
- France
  - www.francogene.com/genealogy/

Europe & Church

- European Records
  - Familysearch.org
  - Catholic
  - Forebears.io

Recommended Genealogy Programs

Windows
Legacy Family Tree

Mac
Gramps

Forms

Family Group Record

 ancestry.com

Prepared By ____________________ Relationship to Preparer ____________________

Address ____________________ Date ____________ Ancestral Chart # ____________ Family Unit # ____________

Husband

Occupation(s) ____________________   Religion ____________________

	Date—Day, Month, Year	City	County	State or Country	
Born					Name of Church
Christened					Name of Church
Married					Cause of Death
Died					Date Will Written/Proved
Buried		Cem/Place			
Father		Other Wives			
Mother					

Wife maiden name

Occupation(s) ____________________   Religion ____________________

Born				Name of Church
Christened				Cause of Death
Died				Date Will Written/Proved
Buried		Cem/Place		
Father		Other Husbands		
Mother				

•	Sex MF	Children Given Names	Birth Day Month Year	Birthplace City	County	St./Ctry.	Date of first marriage/Place Name of Spouse	Date of Death/Cause City County State/Country	Computer I.D. #
		1							
		2							
		3							
		4							
		5							
		6							
		7							
		8							
		9							
		10							
		11							
		12							

NOTE=Direct Ancestor   Form # F106   http://www.ancestry.com/save/charts/familysheet.htm   © 2007 The Generations Network, Inc.

Ancestral Chart

ancestry.com

Chart No. _______

No. 1 on this chart is
the same person as No. _______

On Chart No. _______

BORN
PLACE
MARRIED
PLACE
DIED
PLACE

NAME OF SPOUSE

BORN
PLACE
MARRIED
PLACE
DIED
PLACE

BORN
PLACE
DIED
PLACE

BORN
PLACE
MARRIED
PLACE
DIED
PLACE

BORN
PLACE
DIED
PLACE

BORN
PLACE
MARRIED
PLACE
DIED
PLACE

CONT. ON CHART _______

CONT. ON CHART _______

BORN
PLACE
DIED
PLACE

CONT. ON CHART _______

CONT. ON CHART _______

BORN
PLACE
MARRIED
PLACE
DIED
PLACE

CONT. ON CHART _______

CONT. ON CHART _______

BORN
PLACE
DIED
PLACE

CONT. ON CHART _______

CONT. ON CHART _______

1790 United States Federal Census

 ancestry.com

For more family history charts and forms,
visit www.ancestry.com/save/charts/ancchart.htm

State: _______________ Call Number/URL: _______________

Enumeration Date: _______________

county	city	page	names of heads of families	free white males of 16 years & upwards, including heads of families	free white males under 16 years	free white females including heads of families	all other free persons	slaves

To search the 1790 census online, visit www.ancestry.com

1800 United States Federal Census

ancestry.com

State: _____________ Call Number/URL: _____________ Enumeration Date: _____________

County	County	Page	Names of Heads of Families	Free White Males					Free White Females					All other Free Persons	Slaves
				Under 10	10 thru 15	16 thru 25	26 thru 44	45 and over	Under 10	10 thru 15	16 thru 25	26 thru 44	45 and over		

1810 United States Federal Census

State: _______________ Call Number/URL: _______________ Enumeration Date: _______________

County	County	Page	Names of Heads of Families	Free White Males					Free White Females					All other Free Persons	Slaves
				Under 10	10 thru 15	16 thru 25	26 thru 44	45 and over	Under 10	10 thru 15	16 thru 25	26 thru 44	45 and over		

1820 United States Federal Census

ancestry.com

Page: _______ State: _______ County: _______ Call Number/URL: _______

Enumeration Date: _______

Names of heads of families

Name of the county, parish, township, town, or city where the family resides

Free White Males
- Free white males under ten years (to 10)
- Free white males of ten and under sixteen (10 to 16)
- Free white males between sixteen and eighteen (16 to 18)
- Free white males of sixteen and under twenty-six, including heads of families (16 to 26)
- Free white males of twenty six and under forty-five, including heads of families (26 to 45)
- Free white males of forty five and upwards, including heads of families (45 & c.)

Free White Females
- Free white females under ten years (to 10)
- Free white females of ten and under sixteen (10 to 16)
- Free white females of sixteen and under twenty-six, including heads of families (16 to 26)
- Free white males of twenty six and under forty-five, including heads of families (26 to 45)
- Free white females of forty five and upwards, including heads of families (45 & c.)

Foreigners not naturalized

Numbers of persons engaged in Agriculture

Numbers of persons engaged in Commerce

Numbers of persons engaged in Manufactures

Slaves

Males
- Males under fourteen (to 14)
- Males of fourteen and under twenty-six (to 26)
- Males of twenty-six and under forty-five (to 45)
- Males of forty-five and upwards (45 & c.)

Females
- Females under fourteen (to 14)
- Females of fourteen and under twenty-six (to 26)
- Females of twenty-six and under forty-five (to 45)
- Females of forty-five and upwards (45 & c.)

Free Colored Persons

Males
- Males under fourteen (to 14)
- Males of fourteen and under twenty-six (to 26)
- Males of twenty-six and under forty-five (to 45)
- Males of forty-five and upwards (45 & c.)

Females
- Females under fourteen (to 14)
- Females of fourteen and under twenty-six (to 26)
- Females of twenty-six and under forty-five (to 45)
- Females of forty-five and upwards (45 & c.)

All other persons except Indians not taxed

ancestry.com 1830 United States Federal Census

Page: _______

State: _______   County: _______   Call Number/URL: _______

Enumeration Date: _______

FREE WHITE PERSONS, (INCLUDING HEADS OF FAMILIES).

Males.

Names of Heads of Families / Name of the county, city, ward, town, township, parish, precinct, hundred, or district.	LINE NUMBER	Under five years of age. (under 5)	Of five and under ten. (5 to 10)	Of ten and under fifteen. (10 to 15)	Of fifteen and under twenty. (15 to 20)	Of twenty and under thirty. (20 to 30)	Of thirty and under forty. (30 to 40)	Of forty and under fifty. (40 to 50)	Of fifty and under sixty. (50 to 60)	Of sixty and under seventy. (60 to 70)	Of seventy and under eighty. (70 to 80)	Of eighty and under ninety. (80 to 90)	Of ninety and under one hundred. (90 to 100)	Of one hundred and upward. (100. &c.)

Females.

		Under five years of age. (under 5)	Of five and under ten. (5 to 10)	Of ten and under fifteen. (10 to 15)	Of fifteen and under twenty. (15 to 20)	Of twenty and under thirty. (20 to 30)	Of thirty and under forty. (30 to 40)	Of forty and under fifty. (40 to 50)	Of fifty and under sixty. (50 to 60)	Of sixty and under seventy. (60 to 70)	Of seventy and under eighty. (70 to 80)	Of eighty and under ninety. (80 to 90)	Of ninety and uner one hundred. (90 to 100)	Of one hundred and upward. (100. &c.)

SLAVES AND COLORED PERSONS, included in foregoing.

Who are Deaf and Dumb, under fourteen years of age. (under 14)	Who are Deaf and Dumb, of the age of fourteen and under 25. (14 to 25)	Who are Deaf twenty-five and upwards. (25 &c.)	Who are blind.

WHITE PERSONS included in foregoing.

Who are Deaf and Dumb, under fourteen years of age. (under 14)	Who are Deaf and Dumb, of the age of fourteen and under 25. (14 to 25)	Who are Deaf twenty-five and upwards. (25 &c.)	Who are blind.	ALIENS—Foreigners not naturalized

TOTAL

Freed Colored Persons.

Males. (LINE NUMBER)

Under ten years of age. (under 10)	Of ten and under twenty-four. (10 to 24)	Of twenty-four and under thirty-six. (24 to 36)	Of thirty-six and under fifty-five. (36 to 55)	Of fifty-five and under one hundred. (55 to 100)	Of one hundred and upwards. (100 &c.)

Females.

Under ten years of age. (under 10)	Of ten and under twenty-four. (10 to 24)	Of twenty-four and under thirty-six. (24 to 36)	Of thirty-six and under fifty-five. (36 to 55)	Of fifty-five and under one hundred. (55 to 100)	Of one hundred and upwards. (100 &c.)

Slaves.

Males.

Under ten years of age. (under 10)	Of ten and under twenty-four. (10 to 24)	Of twenty-four and under thirty-six. (24 to 36)	Of thirty-six and under fifty-five. (36 to 55)	Of fifty-five and under one hundred. (55 to 100)	Of one hundred and upwards. (100 &c.)

Females.

Under ten years of age. (under 10)	Of ten and under twenty-four. (10 to 24)	Of twenty-four and under thirty-six. (24 to 36)	Of thirty-six and under fifty-five. (36 to 55)	Of fifty-five and under one hundred. (55 to 100)	Of one hundred and upwards. (100 &c.)

To search the 1830 census online, visit www.ancestry.com

1840 United States Federal Census

Page: _______ State: _______ County: _______ Call Number/URL: _______ Enumeration Date: _______

FREE WHITE PERSONS, (INCLUDING HEADS OF FAMILIES)

LINE NUMBER	Name of the county, city, ward, town, township, parish, precinct, hundred, or district.	Names of Heads of Families	Males.														Females.														Free Colored Persons. Males.						Females.					
			Under 5	5 & under 10	10 & under 15	15 & under 20	20 & under 30	30 & under 40	40 & under 50	50 & under 60	60 & under 70	70 & under 80	80 & under 90	90 & under 100	100 & upwards	Under 5	5 & under 10	10 & under 15	15 & under 20	20 & under 30	30 & under 40	40 & under 50	50 & under 60	60 & under 70	70 & under 80	80 & under 90	90 & under 100	100 & upwards	Under 10	10 & under 24	24 & under 35	36 & under 55	56 & under 100	100 & upwards	Under 10	10 & under 24	24 & under 35	36 & under 55	56 & under 100	100 & upwards

Slaves. / Number of persons in each family employed in / Pensioners for Revolutionary or military services, included in the foregoing. / Deaf and Dumb, Blind, and Insane White Persons, Included in the foregoing / Deaf and Dumb, Blind, and Insane Colored Persons, Included in the foregoing / Schools &c.

LINE NUMBER	Slaves. Males.						Females.						TOTAL	Mining.	Agriculture.	Commerce.	Manufacture and trade.	Navigation of the ocean.	Navigation of canals, lakes, rivers.	Learned professional engineers.	Names (Pensioners)	Ages	Deaf and Dumb			Blind and Insane			Deaf, Dumb, and Blind		Insane and Idiots		Universities or college	Number of students	Academies & Grammar Schools	No. of Scholars	Primary and Common Schools	No. of Scholars at Public charge	No. of white persons over 20 years of age in each family who cannot read and write.
	Under 10	10 & under 24	24 & under 35	36 & under 55	56 & under 100	100 & upwards	Under 10	10 & under 24	24 & under 35	36 & under 55	56 & under 100	100 & upwards											Under 14	14 & under 25	25 & upwards	Blind.	Insane and idiots at public charge.	Insane and idiots at private charge	Deaf & Dumb	Blind.	Insane and idiots at private charge	Insane and idiots at public charge							

1850 United States Federal Census

ancestry.com

Page: ______________ State: ______________ County: ______________ City: ______________
Call Number/URL: ______________ Enumeration Date: ______________

| Dwelling-houses numbered in the order of visitation | Families numbered in the order of visitation | The Name of every Person whose usual place of abode on the first day of June, 1850, was in this family | Description | | | Profession, Occupation or Trade of each Male Person over 15 years of age | Value of Real Estate owned | Place of Birth Naming the State, Territory or County | Married within the year | Attended School within the year | Persons over 20 years of age who cannot read & write | Whether deaf and dumb, blind, insane, idiotic, pauper or convict |
			Age	Sex	Color (White, Black or Mulatto)							
1	2	3	4	5	6	7	8	9	10	11	12	13

1860 United States Federal Census

Page: _______________ State: _______________ County: _______________ City: _______________
Call Number/URL: _______________ Enumeration Date: _______________

Dwelling-houses numbered in the order of visitation	Families numbered in the order of visitation	The Name of every Person whose usual place of abode on the first day of June, 1860, was in this family	Description			Profession, Occupation or Trade of each Male Person over 15 years of age	Value of Real Estate	Value of Personal Estate	Place of Birth Naming the State, Territory or County	Married within the year	Attended School within the year	Persons over 20 years of age who cannot read & write	Whether deaf and dumb, blind, insane, idiotic, pauper or convict
			Age	Sex	Color (White, Black or Mulatto)								
1	2	3	4	5	6	7	8	9	10	11	12	13	14

1870 United States Federal Census

ancestry.com

For more family history charts and forms,
visit www.ancestry.com/save/charts/ancchart.htm

Page: _____________ State: _____________ County: _____________ City: _____________ Call Number/URL: _____________ Enumeration Date: _____________

Dwelling-houses numbered in the order of visitation	Families numbered in the order of visitation	The Name of every Person whose place of abode on the first day of June, 1870, was in this family	Description			Profession, Occupation, or Trade of each Male Person over 15 years of age	Value of Real Estate owned		Place of Birth Naming the State, Territory, or Country	Parentage		If born within the year, state month (Jan, & c.)	If married within the year, state month (Jan, & c.)	Attended School within the year	Education		Whether deaf and dumb, blind, insane, idiotic, pauper, or convict	Constitutional Relations	
			Age at last birth-day. If under 1 year, give months in fractions, thus 3/12	Sex—Male (M), Female (F).	Color—White (W); Black (B); Mulatto (M); Chinese, (C); Indian, (I).		Value of Real Estate	Value of Personal Estate		Father of Foreign born	Mother of Foreign born				Cannot read	Cannot write		Male Citizens of U.S, of 21 years of age and upwards	Male Citizens of U.S, of 21 years of age and upwards where rights to vote is denied on other grounds than rebellion or other crime
1	2	3	4	5	6	7	8	9	10	11	12	13	14	15	16	17	18	19	20

To search the 1870 census online, visit www.ancestry.com

Ancestry Census Form 009

ancestry.com

1880 United States Federal Census

For more family history charts and forms,
visit www.ancestry.com/save/charts/ancchart.htm

State: ______ County: ______ City: ______ Page: ______ E.D.: ______ Call #/URL: ______ Enumeration Date: ______

In Cities											Civil Condition				Occupation			Health					Education			Nativity		
Name of street	House number	Dwelling houses numbered in order of visitation.	Families numbered in order of visitation.	The Name of each Person whose place of abode on 1st day of June 1880, was in this family.	Color—White, W: Black, B: Mulatto, Mu: Chinese, C: Indian, I	Sex—Male, M: Female, F.	Age at last birthday prior to June 1, 1880. If under 1 year, give months in fractions, thus: 8/12	If born within the Census year, give the month.	Relationship of each person to the head of this family—whether wife, son, daughter servant, boarder, or other.	Single	Married	Widowed, divorced	Married during Census year	Profession, Occupation or Trade of each person, male or female.	Numbers of months this person has been unemployed during the Census year.	Is the person (on the day of the enumerator's visit) sick, or temporarily disabled, so as to be unable to attend to ordinary business or duties? If so, what is the sickness or disability?	Blind	Deaf and dumb	Idiotic	Insane	Maimed, crippled, bedridden, or otherwise disabled	Attended school within the Census year.	Cannot read	Cannot write	Place of Birth of this person, naming State or Territory of United States, or the Country if of foreign birth.	Place of Birth of the father of this person, naming State or Territory of United States, or the Country if of foreign birth.	Place of Birth of the mother of this person, naming State or Territory of United States, or the Country if of foreign birth.
		1	2	3	4	5	6	7	8	9	10	11	12	13	14	15	16	17	18	19	20	21	22	23	24	25	26

To search the 1880 census online, visit www.ancestry.com

1890 Veterans Schedule

ancestry.com

State: _______ County: ______________ City/Township: ________________ Call Number/URL: ________________
Enumeration District: ________________ Sheet Number: __________ Enumeration Date: ________________

Line Number	House No.	Family No.	Names of surviving Soldiers, Sailors, Marines and Widows	Rank	Company	Names of regiment or vessel	Date of Enlistment			Date of Discharge			Length of Service			Post Office Address	Disability incurred
							Day	Month	Year	Day	Month	Year	Day	Month	Year		
	1	2	3	4	5	6	7			8			9			10	11

Notes:

1890 United States Federal Census

Ancestry.com

Eleventh Census of the United States.

SCHEDULE NO. 1.
POPULATION AND SOCIAL STATISTICS.

Supervisor's District No. ______________

Enumeration District No. ______________

Name of city, town, township, precinct, district, beat, or other minor civil division. } ______________ County : ______________ State : ______________

Street and No.: ______________ Ward : ________ Name of Institution : ______________

Enumerated by me on the ________ day of June, 1890   ______________
                                                                                                      Enumerator.

A.—Number of **Dwell-ing-house** in the order of visitaion.		B.—Number of families in ths dwelling-house.		C.—Number of persons in this dwelling-house.		D.—Number of **Family** in the order of visitation.		E.—No. of **Persons** in this family.	

INQUIRIES.	1	2	3	4	5
1 Christian name in full, and initial of middle name.					
Surname.					
2 Whether a soldier, sailor, or marine during the civil war (U.S. or Conf.) or widow of such person.					
3 Relationship to head of family.					
4 Whether white, black, mulatto, quadroon, octoroon, Chinese, Japanese, or Indian.					
5 Sex.					
6 Age at nearest birthday. If under one year, give age in months..					
7 Whether single, married, widowed, or divorced.					
8 Whether married during the census year (June 1, 1889, to May 31, 1890.					
9 Mother of how many children, and numer of these children living.					
10 Place of birth.					
11 Place of birth of **Father**.					
12 Place of birth of **Mother**.					
13 Number of years in the United States.					
14 Whether naturalized.					
15 Wheter naturalization papers have been taken out.					
16 Profession, trade, or occupation.					
17 Months employed during the census year (June 1, 1889, to May 31, 1890.					
18 Attendance at school (in months) during the census year (June 1, 1889, to May 31, 1890.					
19 Able to **Read**.					
20 Able to **Write**.					
21 Able to speak English. If not, the language or dialect spoken.					
22 Whether suffering from acute or chronic disease, with name of disease and length of time afflicted.					
23 Whether defective in mind, sight, hearing, or speech, or whether crippled, maimed, or deformed, with name or defect.					
24 Whether a prisoner, convict, homeless child, or pauper.					
25 Supplemental schedule and page.					

TO ENUMERATORS.—See inquiries numbered 26 to 30, inclusive, on the second page of this schedule. These inquiries must be made concerning each family and each farm visited.

1900 United States Federal Census

State: _____________

County: _____________

City, township: _____________

Call Number/URL: _____________

Enumeration District: _____________

Sheet Number: _____________

Enumeration Date: _____________

Line number	Location				Name	Relation	Personal Description									Nativity		
	In Cities		Number of dwelling house in the order of visitation	Number of family, in the order of visitation	of each person whose place of abode on June 1, 1900, was in this family. Enter surname first, then the given name and middle initial, if any. Include every person living on June 1, 1900. Omit children born since June 1, 1900.	Relationship of each person to the head of the family.	Color or Race	Sex	Date of Birth		Age at last birthday	Whether single, married, widowed, or divorced	Number of years of present marriage	Mother of how many children	Number of these children living	Place of birth of each person and parents of each person enumerated. If born in United States, give state or territory. If foreign birth, give the country.		
	Street	House number							Month	Year						Place of birth of this person.	Place of birth of Father of this person.	Place of birth of Mother of this person.
			1	2	3	4	5	6	7		8	9	10	11	12	13	14	15

NOTES:

Line number	Citizenship			Occupation, Trade, or Profession of each person TEN YEARS of age and over.		Education				Ownership of Home				NOTES:
	Year of immigration to the U.S.	Number of years in the U.S.	Naturalization	Occupation	Months not employed	Attended school (in months)	Can read	Can write	Can speak English	Owned or Rented	Owned free or mortgaged	Farm or house	Number of farm schedule	
	16	17	18	19	20	21	22	23	24	25	26	27	28	

ancestry.com

For more family history charts and forms, visit www.ancestry.com/save/charts/ancchart.htm

To search the 1900 census online, visit www.ancestry.com

Ancestry Census Form 012

1910 United States Federal Census

State: _____________ County: _______________ City, township: _______________________________

Call Number/URL: _______________________________

Enumeration District: ___________ Sheet Number: ___________ Enumeration Date: _______________

Location					Name	Relation	Personal Description					Mother of how many children		Nativity			Citizenship	
Line number	Street, avenue, road, etc.	House number or farm	Dwelling Number	Number of family in order of visitation	of each person whose place of abode on April 15, 1910, was in this family. Enter surname first, then the given name and middle initial, if any. Include every person living on April 15, 1910. Omit children born since April 15, 1910.	Relationship of this person to the head of the family	Sex	Color or Race	Age at last birthday	Whether single, married, widowed, or divorced	Number of years of present marriage	Number born	Number now living	Place of birth of this person.	Place of birth of Father of this person.	Place of birth of Mother of this person.	Year of Immigration to the U.S.	Whether naturalized or Alien
			1	2	3	4	5	6	7	8	9	10	11	12	13	14	15	16

Place of birth of each person and parents of each person enumerated. If born in United States, give state or territory. If foreign birth, give the country.

Line number	Whether able to speak English; or, if not, give language spoken.	Occupation			If an employee–		Education			Ownership of Home				Whether a survivor of the Union or Confederate Army or Navy	Whether blind (both eyes)	Whether deaf and dumb
		Trade or profession of, or particular kind of work done by this person.	General nature of industry, business, or establishment in which this person works.	Whether an employer, employee, or working on own account	Whether out of work on April 15, 1910	Number of weeks out of work during 1909	Whether able to read	Whether able to write	Attended school any time since Sept. 1, 1909	Owned or Rented	Owned free or mortgaged	Farm or house	Number of farm schedule			
17		18	19	20	21	22	23	24	25	26	27	28	29	30	31	32

1920 United States Federal Census

State: ___________________ County: ___________________ City / Township: ___________________
Call Number/URL: ___________________ Enumeration District: ___________________ Sheet Number: ___________________ Enumeration Date: ___________________

Line Number	Place of Abode				Name of each person whose place of abode on January 1, 1920 was in this family	Relation	Tenure		Personal Description				Citizenship			Education		
	Street, avenue, road, etc.	House number or farm	Dwelling number	Number of family, in order of visitation		Relationship of this person to the head of the family	Home owned or rented	If owned, free or mortgaged	Sex	Color or Race	Age at last birthday	Single, married, widowed or divorced	Year of immigration to the United States	Naturalized or alien	If naturalized, year of naturalization	Attended school anytime since Sept. 1, 1919	Able to read	Able to write
	1	2	3	4	5	6	7	8	9	10	11	12	13	14	15	16	17	18

Nativity and Mother Tongue

Place of birth of each person and parents of each person enumerated. If born in the United States, give state or territory. If foreign birth, give the place of birth, and, in addition, the mother tongue.

Line Number	Person		Father		Mother		Able to speak english	Occupation			No. of farm schedule
	Place of Birth	Mother Tongue	Place of Birth	Mother Tongue	Place of Birth	Mother Tongue		Trade, profession or particular kind of work done	Industry, business or establishment of work done	Employer, salary or wage worker, or working on own account	
	19	20	21	22	23	24	25	26	27	28	29

To search the 1920 census online. visit www.ancestry.com

1930 United States Federal Census

State: _____________

County: _____________

City, township: _____________

Call Number/URL: _____________

Enumeration District: _____________

Sheet Number: _____________

Enumeration Date: _____________

Line number	PLACE OF ABODE				NAME	RELATION	HOME DATA				PERSONAL DESCRIPTION					EDUCATION		PLACE OF BIRTH		
	Street, avenue, road, etc.	House number (in cities or towns)	Number of dwelling house in order of visitation	Number of family in order of visitation	of each person whose place of abode on April 1, 1930, was in this family. Enter surname first, then the given name and middle intitial, if any. Include every person living on April 1, 1930. Omit children born since April 1, 1930.	Relationship of this person to the head of the family	Home owned or rented	Value of home, if owned, or monthly rental, if rented	Radio set	Does this family live on a farm?	Sex	Color or race	Age at last birthday	Marital condition	Age at first marriage	Attended school or college any time since Sept.1,1929	Whether able to read and write	Place of birth of each person and parents of each person enumerated. If born in the United States, give the State or Territory. If of foreign birth, give the country of birth. See Instructions for additional entries required for certain countries		
																		PERSON	FATHER	MOTHER
	1	2	3	4	5	6	7	8	9	10	11	12	13	14	15	16	17	18	19	20

Line number	MOTHER TONGUE (OR NATIVE LANGUAGE) OF FOREIGN BORN				CITIZENSHIP			OCCUPATION AND INDUSTRY				EMPLOYMENT		VETERANS		No. of farm schedule	NOTES:
	Language spoken in home before coming to the United States	CODE (For office use only. Do not write in these columns)			Year of immigration to the United States	Naturalized or alien	Whether able to speak English	OCCUPATION Trade, profession, or particular kind of work, as spinner, salesman, riveter, etc.	INDUSTRY Industry or business, as cottonmill, dry goods store, shipyard, public school, etc.	CODE (For office use only. Do not write in this column)	Class of Worker	Whether actually at work		Whether a veteran of the U.S. military or naval forces mobilized for any war or expedition			
		State or M.T	Country									Yes or No	Line number for unemployed	Yes or No	What war or expedition		
	21	A	B	C	22	23	24	25	26	D	27	28	29	30	31	32	

To search the census online, visit www.ancestry.com

ancestry.com

Ancestry Census Form 015

State ....

County ....

Incorporated place ....

Township or other division of county ....

Ward of city...

Unincorporated place ....
(Name of unincorporated place having 100 or more inhabitants)

Block Nos...

Institution ....
(Name of institution and lines on which entries are made)

SIXTE...

Line No.	LOCATION		HOUSEHOLD DATA				NAME	RELATION	PERSONAL DESCRIPTION					EDUCATION			PLACE OF BIRTH		CITIZENSHIP		RESIDENCE, APRIL 1, 1935		
	Street, avenue, road, etc.	House number (in cities and towns)	Number of household in order of visitation	Home owned (O) or rented (R)	Value of home, if owned, or monthly rental, if rented	Does this household live on a farm? (Yes or No)	Name of each person whose *usual place of residence* on April 1, 1940, was in this household. BE SURE TO INCLUDE: 1. Persons temporarily absent from household. Write "Ab" after names of such persons. 2. Children under 1 year of age. Write "Infant" if child has not been given a first name. Enter "X" after name of person furnishing information.	Relationship of this person to the head of the household, as wife, daughter, father, mother-in-law, grandson, lodger, lodger's wife, servant, hired hand, etc.	CODE (Leave blank)	Sex - Male (M), Female (F)	Color or race	Age at last birthday	Marital Status - Single (S), Married (M) Widowed (Wd), Divorced (D)	Attended school or college any time since March 1, 1940? (Yes or No)	Highest grade of school completed	CODE (Leave blank)	If born in the United States, give State, Territory, or possession. If foreign born, give country in which birthplace was situated on January 1, 1937. Distinguish Canada-French from Canada-English and Irish Free State (Eire) from Northern Ireland.	CODE (Leave blank)	Citizenship of the foreign born	City, town, or village having 2,500 or more inhabitants. Enter "R" for all other places.	COUNTY	STATE (or Territory or foreign country)
	1	2	3	4	5	6	7	8	A	9	10	11	12	13	14	B	15	C	16	17	18	19
1																						
2																						
3																						
4																						
5																						
6																						
7																						
8																						
9																						
10																						
11																						
12																						
13																						
SUPPL. QUEST. 14																						
15																						
16																						
17																						
18																						
19																						
20																						
21																						
22																						
23																						
24																						
25																						
26																						
27																						
28																						
SUPPL. QUEST. 29																						
30																						
31																						
32																						
33																						
34																						
35																						
36																						
37																						
38																						
39																						
40																						

Check, if household cont. on next page ☐

SUPPLEMENTARY QUESTIONS

For Persons Enumerated on Lines 14 and 29

FOR PERSONS OF ALL AGES

FOR PERSONS 14 YEARS OL...

Line No.	NAME	PLACE OF BIRTH OF FATHER AND MOTHER		MOTHER TONGUE (OR NATIVE LANGUAGE)		VETERANS			SOCIAL SECURITY			USUAL OCCUPATION, I...	U...
		If born in the United States, give State, Territory, or possession. If foreign born, give country in which birthplace was situated on January 1, 1937 Distinguish Canada-French from Canada-English and Irish Free State (Eire) from Northern Ireland		Language spoken in home in earliest childhood		Is this person a veteran of the United States military forces; or the wife, widow, or under 18-year-old child of a veteran?			Does this person have a Social Security Number? (Yes or No)			Enter that occupation which the person reg... able to work. If the person is unable to dete... longest during the past 10 year... Enter also usual ind... For a person without previous... leave C...	
		FATHER	MOTHER		CODE (Leave blank)		CODE (Leave blank)	If so, enter "Yes"	If child, is veteran-father (Yes or No)	War or military service	CODE (Leave blank)	Were deductions for Federal Old-Age Insurance or Railroad Retirement made from this person's wages or salary?	If so, were deductions made from (1) all, (2) one-half or more, (3) part, but less than half?	USUAL OCCUPATION	U...
	35	36	37	G	38	H	39	40	41	I	42	43	44	45
14														
29														

SYMBOLS AND EXPLANATORY NOTES

COL. 5. VALUE OF HOME, IF OWNED: Where owner's household occupies only a part of a structure, estimate value of portion occupied by owner's household. Thus the value of the unit occupied by the owner of a two-family house might be approximately one-half the total value of the structure.

COL. 10. COLOR OR RACE:
White .... W
Negro .... Neg
Indian .... In
Chinese .... Chi
Japanese .... Jp
Filipino .... Fil
Hindu .... Hin
Korean .... Kor
Other race, spell out in full.

COL. 11. AGE AT LAST BIRTHDAY: Enter age of children born on or after April 1, 1939, as follows. Born in:
April 1939 .... 11/12
May 1939 .... 10/12
June 1939 .... 9/12
July 1939 .... 8/12
August 1939 .... 7/12
September 1939 .... 6/12
October 1939 .... 5/12
November 1939 .... 4/12
December 1939 .... 3/12
January 1939 .... 2/12
February 1939 .... 1/12
March 1939 .... 0/12
(Do not include children born on or after April 1, 1940.)

COL. 14. HIGHEST GRADE OF SCHOOL COMPLETED:
None C
Elementary school, 1st to 9th grade .... 1, 2, et., to 8
High school, 1st to 4th year H-1, H-2, H-3, H-4
College, 1st to 4th year C-1, C-2, C-3, C-4
College, 5th or subsequent year C-5

COL. 16. CITI...
Natural...
Having...
Alien...
Americ...

DEPARTMENT OF COMMERCE-BUREAU OF THE CENSUS

SIXTEENTH CENSUS OF THE UNITED STATES: 1940

POPULATION SCHEDULE

S. D. No. .... E. D. No. ....

Sheet No. **A**

Enumerated by me on ...., 1940

...., Enumerator.

.... rated place having 100 or more inhabitants)

.... ion and lines on which entries are made)

CITIZEN-SHIP	RESIDENCE, APRIL 1, 1935						PERSONS 14 YEARS OLD AND OVER—EMPLOYMENT STATUS								OCCUPATION, INDUSTRY, AND CLASS OF WORKER					INCOME IN 1939 (12 months ending December 31, 1939)			
Citizenship of the foreign born	City, town, or village having 2,500 or more inhabitants. Enter "R" for all other places.	COUNTY	STATE (or Territory or foreign country)	On a farm? (Yes or No)	CODE (Leave blank)	Was this person AT WORK for pay or profit in private or even-emergency Gov't. work during week of March 24-30? (Yes or No)	If not, was he at work on, or assigned to, public EMERGENCY WORK (WPA, NYA, CCC, etc.) during week of March 24-30? (Yes or No)	Was this person SEEKING WORK? (Yes or No)	If not seeking work, did he HAVE A JOB, business, etc.? (Yes or No)	Indicate whether engaged in home housework (H), in school (S), unable to work (U) or other (O)	CODE	Number of hours worked during week of March 24-30, 1940	Duration of unemployment up to March 30, 1940—in weeks	OCCUPATION Trade, profession, or particular kind of work, as - frame spinner salesman laborer rivet heater music teacher	INDUSTRY Industry or business, as - cotton mill retail grocery farm shipyard public school	Class of worker	CODE (Leave blank)	Number of weeks worked in 1939 (Equivalent full-time weeks)	Amount of money wages or salary received (including commissions)	Did this person receive income of $50 or more from sources other than money wages or salary? (Yes or No)	Number of Farm Schedule	Line No.
16	17	18	19	20	D	21	22	23	24	25	E	26	27	28	29	30	F	31	32	33	34	
																						1
																						2
																						3
																						4
																						5
																						6
																						7
																						8
																						9
																						10
																						11
																						12
																						13
																						14 SUPPL. QUEST.
																						15
																						16
																						17
																						18
																						19
																						20
																						21
																						22
																						23
																						24
																						25
																						26
																						27
																						28
																						29 SUPPL. QUEST.
																						30
																						31
																						32
																						33
																						34
																						35
																						36
																						37
																						38
																						39
																						40

IN WHAT PLACE DID THIS PERSON LIVE ON APRIL 1, 1935?

For a person who, on April 1, 1935, was living in the same house as at present, enter in Col. 17 "Same house," and for one living in a different house but in the same city or town, enter, "Same place," leaving Cols. 18, 19, and 20 blank, in both instances.

For a person who lived in a different place, enter city or town, county, and State, as directed in the instructions. (Enter actual place of residence, which may differ from mail address.)

	SOCIAL SECURITY			FOR PERSONS 14 YEARS OLD AND OVER				FOR ALL WOMEN WHO ARE OR HAVE BEEN MARRIED			FOR OFFICE USE ONLY - DO NOT WRITE IN THESE COLUMNS													
Does this person have a Federal Social Security Number? (Yes or No)	Were deductions for Federal Old-Age Insurance or Railroad Retirement made from this person's wages or salary in 1939?	If so, were deductions made from (1) all, (2) one-half or more, or (3) part, but less than one-half, of wages or salary?	USUAL OCCUPATION	USUAL INDUSTRY	Usual class of worker	CODE (Leave blank)		Has this woman been married more than once? (Yes or No)	Age at first marriage	Number of children ever born (Do not include stillbirths)	Ten (4)	V-R (5)	Fm. res, and Sex (6 and 9)	Color and (10, 15, 56, and 37)	Age (11)	Mar. st. (12)	Gr. Com. (8)	Cit. (16)	Wrk. st. (E)	Hrs. wkd. or Dur. un. (26 or 27)	Occupation, industry, and class of worker (F)	Wks. wkd. (31)	Wages (32)	Ot. Inc. (33)	Line No.
42	43	44	45	46	47	J	48	49	50	K	L	M	N	O	P	Q	R	S	T	U	V	W	X	Y	Z	
																										14
																										29

USUAL OCCUPATION, INDUSTRY, AND CLASS OF WORKER

Enter that occupation which the person regards as his usual occupation and at which he is physically able to work. If the person is unable to determine this, enter that occupation at which he has worked longest during the past 10 years and at which he is physically able to work.

Enter also usual industry and usual class of worker.

For a person without previous work experience, enter "None" in Col. 45 and leave Cols. 46 and 47 blank.

L. 14. HIGHEST GRADE OF SCHOOL COMPLETED:

None	C
Elementary school, 1st to 8th grade	1,2,et., to 8
High school, 1st to 4th year	H-1, H-2, H-3, H-4
College, 1st to 4th year	C-1, C-2, C-3, C-4
College, 5th or subsequent year	C-5

COL. 16. CITIZENSHIP OF THE FOREIGN BORN:

Naturalized	Na
Having first papers	Pa
Alien	Al
American citizen born abroad	Am Cit

COL. 21. WAS THIS PERSON AT WORK?

Enter "Yes" for persons at work for pay or profit in private or nonemergency Goverment work. Include unpaid family workers – that is, family working without money wages or salary on work (other than house work or incidental chores) which contributed to the family income.

COL. 24. DID THIS PERSON HAVE A JOB?

Enter "Yes" for person (not seeking work) who had a job, business, or professional enterprise, but did not work during week of March 24-30 for any of the following reason: Vacation; temporary illness; industrial dispute; layoff not exceeding 4 weeks with instructions to return to work at a specific date; layoff due to temporarily bad weather conditions.

COLS. 30 AND 47. CLASS OF WORKER:

Wage or salary worker in private work	PW
Wage or salary worker in Government work	GW
Employer	E
Working on own account	OA
Unpaid family worker	NP

COL. 41. WAR OR MILITARY SERVICE:

World War	W
Spanish-American War, Philippine Insurrection, or Boxer Rebellion	S
Spanish-American War and World War	SW
Regular establishment (Army, Navy, or Marine Corps) peace-time service only	R
Other war or expedition	Ot

1850 Slave Schedule

Schedule 2.-Slave Inhabitants in________________________ ______ in the County of __________________ State of____________ , enumerated by me, on the ________ day of ______________, 1850 ____________ Ass't Marchal.

| NAMES OF SLAVE OWNERS | Number of Slaves | DESCRIPTION | | | Fugitives from the State | Number manumitted | Deaf & Dumb, blind, insane or idiotic |
		Age	Sex	Color			
1	2	3	4	5	6	7	8
1							
2							
3							
4							
5							
6							
7							
8							
9							
10							

| NAMES OF SLAVE OWNERS | Number of Slaves | DESCRIPTION | | | Fugitives from the State | Number manumitted | Deaf & Dumb, blind, insane or idiotic |
		Age	Sex	Color			
1	2	3	4	5	6	7	8
1							
2							
3							
4							
5							
6							
7							
8							
9							
10							

African Americans in the Federal Censuses

African Americans were enumerated in the census as all other U.S. residents from 1870 (the first census year following the Civil War and emancipation) onward. Prior to 1870, however, the situation was far different. Although free African Americans were enumerated by name in 1850 and 1860, slaves were consigned to special, far less informative, schedules in which they were listed anonymously under the names of their owners. The only personal information provided was usually that of age, gender, and racial identity (either black or mulatto). As in the free schedules, there was a column in which certain physical or mental infirmities could be noted. In some instances, the census takers noted an occupation, usually carpenter or blacksmith, in this column. Slaves aged 100 years or more were given special treatment; their names were noted, and sometimes a short biographical sketch was included. In at least one instance, that of 1860 Hampshire County, Virginia, the names of all slaves were included on the schedules, but this happy exception may be the only instance when the instructions were not followed.

Sometimes the listings for large slaveholdings appear to take the form of family groupings, but in most cases slaves are listed from eldest to youngest with no apparent effort to portray family structure. In any event, the slave schedules themselves almost never provide conclusive evidence for the presence of a specific slave in the household or plantation of a particular slaveowner. At best, a census slave schedule can provide supporting evidence for a hypothesis derived from other sources.[1] Prior to 1850 there were no special slave schedules for the manuscript census, as slave data was recorded as part of the general population schedules. In these, only the heads of household were enumerated by name.

In the absence of any contradictory information, it might be assumed that a family of freed people enumerated in the 1870 census was living not far from its last owner, whose surname they also bore. There would, of course, be reasons to dispute both assumptions. (Knowledge of the Civil War history of a locality could come into play here; for example, such relative stability would not have existed in a Georgia county that was in the path of Sherman's march to the sea.) Even so, this assumption represents one of the more obvious exploratory lines of research, especially in the absence of any other options. The first step in testing the hypothesis would be to search for slaveowners of the same surname in the 1860 slave schedules of the county in which the African American family resided in 1870.

Starting in 1850, another supplemental schedule, the mortality schedule, listed all deaths within a year before the regular census enumeration.[2] The deaths of blacks and mulattoes, both free and slave, are recorded in them, even though their names have not been included in many of the indexes to these schedules.[3] The deaths of slaves were generally enumerated in four fashions: unnamed (as in the slave schedules), but perhaps with the owner identified; by first name only; by first name and surname; and by first name with the owner noted.

Notes

1. The use of the slave schedules as supporting documentation is amply demonstrated in David H. Streets, Slave Genealogy: A Research Guide with Case Studies (Bowie, MD: Heritage, 1986), although, not surprisingly, their use is confined to small slaveholdings.

2. See Loretto Dennis Szucs, "Research in Census Records" in The Source: A Guidebook of American Genealogy, Rev. ed. (Salt Lake City, UT: Ancestry, 1997).

3. A notable exception is found in Jonnie B. Arnold, Index to 1860 Mortality Schedule of South Carolina (Greenville, SC: the author, 1982). On the other hand, many of the indexes appearing on the National Archives microfilm publications of these schedules, as well as those published by Accelerated Indexing, should be treated with caution.

Editor's Note: This article was excerpted from Finding Your African American Ancestors, by David Thackery. Other sources covered in the book include: probate records; deeds and other local records; plantation records; other records of slave births and deaths; runaway slaves; The Bureau of Refugees, Freedmen, and Abandoned Lands; The Freedman's Savings and Trust; and military records. Also included are case studies, a selection of slave narratives from a variety of states, bibliographic information, and an extensive listing of additional resources for African American research.

1860 Slave Schedule

Page No. _______

Schedule 2.-Slave Inhabitants in_________________________________ in the County of __________________ State
of____________ , enumerated by me, on the _________ day of _______________, 1860____________ Ass't Marchal.

NAMES OF SLAVE OWNERS	Number of Slaves	DESCRIPTION			Fugitives from the State	Number manumitted	Deaf & Dumb, blind, insane or idiotic	No. of Slave Houses	NAMES OF SLAVE OWNERS	Number of Slaves	DESCRIPTION			Fugitives from the State	Number manumitted	Deaf & Dumb, blind, insane or idiotic	No. of Slave Houses
		Age	Sex	Color							Age	Sex	Color				
1	2	3	4	5	6	7	8	9	1	2	3	4	5	6	7	8	9
1																	
2																	
3																	
4																	
5																	
6																	
7																	
8																	
9																	
10																	

African Americans in the Federal Censuses

African Americans were enumerated in the census as all other U.S. residents from 1870 (the first census year following the Civil War and emancipation) onward. Prior to 1870, however, the situation was far different. Although free African Americans were enumerated by name in 1850 and 1860, slaves were consigned to special, far less informative, schedules in which they were listed anonymously under the names of their owners. The only personal information provided was usually that of age, gender, and racial identity (either black or mulatto). As in the free schedules, there was a column in which certain physical or mental infirmities could be noted. In some instances, the census takers noted an occupation, usually carpenter or blacksmith, in this column. Slaves aged 100 years or more were given special treatment; their names were noted, and sometimes a short biographical sketch was included. In at least one instance, that of 1860 Hampshire County, Virginia, the names of all slaves were included on the schedules, but this happy exception may be the only instance when the instructions were not followed.

Sometimes the listings for large slaveholdings appear to take the form of family groupings, but in most cases slaves are listed from eldest to youngest with no apparent effort to portray family structure. In any event, the slave schedules themselves almost never provide conclusive evidence for the presence of a specific slave in the household or plantation of a particular slaveowner. At best, a census slave schedule can provide supporting evidence for a hypothesis derived from other sources.[1] Prior to 1850 there were no special slave schedules for the manuscript census, as slave data was recorded as part of the general population schedules. In these, only the heads of household were enumerated by name.

In the absence of any contradictory information, it might be assumed that a family of freed people enumerated in the 1870 census was living not far from its last owner, whose surname they also bore. There would, of course, be reasons to dispute both assumptions. (Knowledge of the Civil War history of a locality could come into play here; for example, such relative stability would not have existed in a Georgia county that was in the path of Sherman's march to the sea.) Even so, this assumption represents one of the more obvious exploratory lines of research, especially in the absence of any other options. The first step in testing the hypothesis would be to search for slaveowners of the same surname in the 1860 slave schedules of the county in which the African American family resided in 1870.

Starting in 1850, another supplemental schedule, the mortality schedule, listed all deaths within a year before the regular census enumeration.[2] The deaths of blacks and mulattoes, both free and slave, are recorded in them, even though their names have not been included in many of the indexes to these schedules.[3] The deaths of slaves were generally enumerated in four fashions: unnamed (as in the slave schedules), but perhaps with the owner identified; by first name only; by first name and surname; and by first name with the owner noted.

Notes

1. The use of the slave schedules as supporting documentation is amply demonstrated in David H. Streets, *Slave Genealogy: A Research Guide with Case Studies* (Bowie, MD: Heritage, 1986), although, not surprisingly, their use is confined to small slaveholdings.

2. See Loretto Dennis Szucs, "Research in Census Records" in *The Source: A Guidebook of American Genealogy*, Rev. ed. (Salt Lake City, UT: Ancestry, 1997).

3. A notable exception is found in Jonnie B. Arnold, *Index to 1860 Mortality Schedule of South Carolina* (Greenville, SC: the author, 1982). On the other hand, many of the indexes appearing on the National Archives microfilm publications of these schedules, as well as those published by Accelerated Indexing, should be treated with caution.

Editor's Note: This article was excerpted from Finding Your African American Ancestors, by David Thackery. Other sources covered in the book include: probate records; deeds and other local records; plantation records; other records of slave births and deaths; runaway slaves; The Bureau of Refugees, Freedmen, and Abandoned Lands; The Freedman's Savings and Trust; and military records. Also included are case studies, a selection of slave narratives from a variety of states, bibliographic information, and an extensive listing of additional resources for African American research.